SHED

M.G. Sprinkle

BookLeaf Publishing

India | USA | UK

Presentation by *BookLeaf Publishing*

Web: www.bookleafpub.com

E-mail: info@bookleafpub.com

ISBN: 9789358319057

First edition 2023

DEDICATION

For my family and friends. You always knew I could
do it, and you never let me doubt myself.

Excavations

Do you think bones ever get lonely
waiting centuries upon centuries
for some coffee-fueled khaki-wearer
to dig them up and pronounce them interesting,
if not by deed or race or station, then by
the incredible mundanity that is old age?

Do you think they lie there—the last of
their kind, the humble farmer, the blessed
Mother curled 'round her child—just
waiting for the day when they will be found?
I remember reading an archaeologist say
they determined the difference between
rocks and bones by licking them.
Rock-dirt and bone-dirt taste different,
and it's a thin line between being discarded
or being marked as worthy of exploration.
All those lost souls under the crushing earth
craving love and sunlight once more,
value determined with a kiss and yet,
when they are pulled from dust fractured
or fully formed, it is with gloved hands.

When I was a child, I was obsessed with
Egyptology. We had just moved into a
new house where the grass had not yet been
laid down. I would beg my mother for an old
makeup brush and any pieces of hard plastic

we had lying around. Then, armed with a spade,
I took my tools out to the sandy plot and buried
my treasures. Soon after, I would dig them back up,
treating mostly-empty lipstick tubes and stray rocks
and stiff plastic rings that hold soda bottles together
as precious as the undiscovered tomb entrance
for a Pharaoh. On my hands and knees in jeans shorts
and a tank top, I used the makeup brush and my
breath to reveal these sacred items, clearing the dirt
and clay away as gently as I dared. They were so
fragile, as brittle as bones from a thousand years
ago, and I imagined myself as those archaeologists
on TV, describing the history of each find with a
reverence usually reserved for church pews.
I held the lipstick tube, and I whispered to it
of a history I created, connecting the items and
connecting to them with hands ungloved.

At the time, I did not recognize the yearning
in me to have someone interested enough
to dig up my history, be gentle with what
remained, and proclaim it holy.

What I Would go Back for

There was a fire at my complex
a few years back, and I didn't know
which apartment was in flames.
No one was there, not even my pets,
but I rushed home all the same.
It is said that fire reveals our priorities,
our most precious of possessions, so
it makes sense that all I could think
about were my books. Hundreds of
stories I'd read and reread countless
times, loving them to fragility. Their
spines were cracked, pages thin and
brittle from the oil of my fingers.
Some were annotated on every page.
I knew they could be replaced, and
I was relieved to find out it was not
my home that burned, that no one was hurt,
but to me, their value was incalculable.
The mere thought was enough to make
me weep for what could have been lost.
It was enough to make me realize that I
would have gone back for them. I worry
that I would have stayed with them.

I think of the Library of Alexandria, caught
ablaze in a pursuit of power and filling
the air with smoke, and I think that they too,
would understand how someone could rush

back inside the building. All that knowledge,
all those stories… It's impossible to save them all,
but I can't bear the thought of them burning alone.

This is How I Take Care of Myself

I.

I have 21 meal vouchers per week;
14 of them remain unused. That's
7 breakfasts, 2 lunches, 5 dinners forsaken.
I make mac'n'cheese in the microwave
and some days, it's the only thing I eat
if I eat anything at all.
I do not think this is a problem.
I call it focus, I call it laziness, I call
myself forgetful even as my belly
twists in an empty corkscrew.
I call it everything but what it is. No
one knows me here and the last
thing I want them to see is some
out-of-towner fat girl who only
wears leggings because her jeans
fit on the ugly side of too tight.

II.

The first week, I wake up at 7 AM
even on the weekends, in some
attempt at independence, some
play at adulthood. Going out for
a walk, check out the farmers market,

grab a giant slice of pizza down the road.
See, Mom? I'm getting out. I'm doing
things. I'm part of the community.
I love it here; I'm having a great time.
I'm making friends and making you proud.

My life boils down to filtered Instagram
posts, pictures taken weeks before I share
them, because I haven't done things like that
since my first month away from home.

III.

I face-time with my boyfriend, or
at least call him every night. Our
relationship is still fairly new and
I am terrified that he will realize
I'm not the kind of girl he wants
a long-distance relationship with.
Maybe I'm not the kind of girl he
wants a relationship with. My flaws
become my roommate, whispering to
me in the dark. I stay
awake, tossing and turning,
unable to disregard all the scenarios
created where he leaves me, calls
me up and with the sound of his
voice I know what is coming.

I cry myself to sleep more often
than I would like to admit.

IV.

It's 1 AM, 42 degrees, and I have
2 essays to finish. I've had 5
cups of hot tea because my window
is broken and the cold Virginia air creeps in.
1 blanket is draped over my shoulders,
another burying my feet, and still
my toes are frozen and tingling.
My mom gave me her unused
surgery pills to help with my
migraines and these essays are
bringing one on. Or so I tell myself.
I pop 2 because 1 does nothing,
wait 23 minutes exactly
until my surroundings go smooth.
I stop feeling the numbness of my
extremities. I exit my own head,
and my fingers fly over the keyboard.
2 essays finished in record time.
Finally, I curl up in bed, sweating in the
cold, waiting for my skin to start itching,
my fingers to twitch, and I lay awake
through the high until it wears off
4 hours later. I take 2 more because
feeling everything and nothing at once
is better than the loneliness pervading
all that is outside of the pills.
She is colder than the winter wind
that killed my rosebuds and gardenia,
that sneaks into my bed and pinches my skin
until I wake up with bruises the next

morning, that makes me write down
all the ways in which I am a disappointment
so I can read them later, plagued by the
cruelty of my own words.
I sell a couple of pills to a classmate
so I can buy more macaroni
that I'm not going to eat. Just
another way for me to self-destruct.

V.

The end of the semester brings
on an illness I cannot shake.
I cry when I tell my Shakespeare
professor that I won't be able to
make it to class. My fever is 104.2
and I am terrified that she won't
understand. I'm so weak that
I can't climb in bed, so I pass
out on the floor with the minifridge
door open, right in front of my face.
My cultural studies professor sets
up a meeting with me due to the
classes I've missed. I cry there too,
even as he tells me to put my health
first, but I don't know how to do
that. It's the grades that matter:
Top of the class, best in show, pin
a ribbon on the milky white pig.
I never learned to value myself above
my success, so I drag myself to
Urgent Care, a caricature of self-preservation,

and vomit up my antibiotics amid
scrambling to turn in my final
assignments. I'm sick for a month,
lose my voice entirely, text with my
family and tell them I'm busy with
homework and can't talk on the phone
right now. They praise me for doing
such a good job, and I preen underneath
their pride. It's all I've ever wanted.

When my mom visits to help me
drive home for winter break, I see
the shock on her face quickly schooled.
It's impossible to hide that I am still
gray with fever. I have 19 unused meal vouchers,
and the little bookshelf for snacks in my
room is filled with mac'n'cheese.
I'm out of pills; my head is aching.
I just need the world to smooth out,
because I can't operate under her perceptive
gaze. But Mom, aren't you proud of me?
My sleep shorts are loose on my hips,
I have straight A's, and I've never looked better.

Capacity to Punish

Sometimes, I play a little game with myself.
I map out conversations as if they were a
chess match, crafting my response to your
reply, anticipating the calculated slide of
your bishop, the jump of your knight.
Did you know the average chess game
has 10 to the 120th power possible moves
and outcomes? I've played out every combination
baby, I'm a Grand Master. I know just how
you would hurt me, and I know how
to make you.

My thumb hovers over self-destruct,
waiting for the day when I collapse
on the button like a severed marionette.
Would you leave quietly, a silent packing
of your things before driving away?
Would you put up a fight, try to fix it,
make me communicate like you always do?
It's no use. The game is over. We've played out all
the things to say in this match. Maybe you
would tell me you knew this was coming.
That I was spiraling, that I had catastrophe
burning my mouth like an ember. My tongue
is scarred from all that I've said. I imagine
you tell me that you knew from the start
we were doomed. I loved too fast, too much.
I was too trusting of my plucked heartstrings.

How naïve.

You don't have to tell me any of this—I already
know. I know what you'll say, the exact
timbre of your voice, unshaken. You're so
steady, unflappable. Maybe I'm just looking
for a reaction from you. It seems unfair that
I'm the only one visibly suffering. I have bad
habits too. One of these days, I might over-
indulge. Give you something that would make
you disapprove. Things that would worry you.
Give me an excuse to lie to you and say I'm fine.
Let the sins stack upon one another in a crooked
tower. It's no wonder it toppled. Everyone knew
it was going to happen sooner or later.

Of course, I do none of these, but my thumb
still trembles over the button with the effort
of staying still. You don't register the weight
of your arm until you keep it suspended, and
it feels like I've been standing like this for
years. It would be so easy to press down. Such
a relief to relax my hand and drop my arm.
Sometimes, my capacity to punish myself
surprises me.

On Funerals

you didn't even want to come to this
spent the entire flight thinking about how
you didn't need to be there
but your family asked and you're a pushover
so you came anyway against your better judgment
because you knew this would happen
you knew it would be awkward and weird and
too quiet
then too loud
too much crying too little conversation about
anything except the cold woman in a box at
the front of the room that you are clearly avoiding
hanging around the back like a leper
hands in your pockets because you're not interested
in touching the others
hugging them
and saying you miss her too even though you do
like a wound reopened
your palms raked across cut glass and fingernails
digging
into the slices
you miss her like something has been taken from you
chipped away with doctors' visits and
breathless phone calls and
forgetting your fucking name
but it's fine
you're here and it's fine
you came because they asked

because they needed you
and your family is uneducated in everything
except a dangerous vein of codependency
that knocks at your own door
uneducated in everything except
how to love each other with the whole of your being
like suffocating but you asked for it
like drowning when you're parched
like saying you're cold and they soak you in gasoline
set you on fire and you can't do anything but
thank them because *god*
you're finally warm again
and you stand at the back of the room until your
father
pulls your hand from your pocket and leads you
to his mom
and you hold your breath the whole way because
she looks so brown and warm like
she's sleeping
like she's going to pop up any second and ask you
if you're hungry
and every step takes you closer
to the torn heart you've duct taped to your chest
where the volume of missing her is a speaker
that can't be turned down and if you add
your own voice to the song
the building will crumble
so you whisper goodbye and hope it's loud enough
because it's expected
because he's holding your hand but he's the one
shaking
as you stand before her

the empty shell of a woman whose insides ate at her
like yours are eating away at you now
hungry for your own pain
hungry to heal the hurt of another because
you can take it
but disease spits in the face of altruism
and you're not strong you're just there
you're holding him up as you lead him away
you set yourself aside and become the backbone
the cane
the rhythm that keeps the music on beat
beats at your back until your teeth are grinding
you step away from the need
from the storm of your father
when your own is a hurricane
you step outside into the sunshine
into the heat
and can't catch your breath
can't do anything until you turn it off
because you can't be what everyone else needs
the pillar of strength and understanding
if you remain yourself

Cycles

They never tell you all the rules.
They say you're too young to understand,
but they don't want to explain it when
you're older for fear that you will act
upon the knowledge. They tiptoe around the
words, unable to describe what they tell
you not to be ashamed of, so how
are we to be blamed for discovering
our own bodies and each other's?

Learn just enough so you aren't
a stranger to the mechanics, but if you think
about it too much it's wrong. Don't go looking
for more details either, or you'll find things
disapproved of. Treat it as something
sacred, which means, don't ever
talk about it with anyone. It's an
inappropriate topic. But tell someone if it
happens against your will. Just don't tell them
what you were wearing, because that will end up
mattering more than anything else. Don't
invite trouble by looking at the nakedness
of others, and don't look at your own nakedness.
Avert your gaze, for fear of seeing something
valuable.

They call it private, they call it special,
and if you get it all out of order they call you

a whore. You're no longer "so smart
for your age," you're just a dumb kid
who didn't know what they were doing,
and now you have to live with the mistakes
you made. Damaged goods walking around,
donning shame like an heirloom so heavy you
can't wait to pass it on to your own daughter.
We are given the key to a door with
one of the most special experiences
of our life on the other side. How can we be
vilified for unlocking it?

All or Nothing

You get in these phases where
you like to mix drinks
no flair but measured pours
and I like to watch you
because I like looking at you
and you look so pleased with
yourself when it's good

You ask if I want a sip
just a taste
and I decline
are you sure
and I decline
you offer to make me whatever I want
And I do want
but I always decline
I know how I get
I open the bottle of wine
and finish it the same night
making excuses about the carbonation
because I like 'em sweet and fizzy
and it's not the same if it goes flat
or I have half a glass and waste the rest
not really in the mood but the bottle
was staring at me
and it will keep staring
sitting in the fridge and mocking me
I hear it say my name everytime

I open the door

The same bottle of gin
has been sitting on the shelf for years
it's not even half-empty
no one else drinks it but me
bought on a whim because I did what
I always do
I find a drink I like and I can't
think of anything else
and I need one or three or five everyday
until I realize what I'm doing
so the guilt of having it sit there
untouched grows heavy
it's a little hidden by other liquors
vodka and rum and whiskey
but the sapphire blue winks at me
catches my attention like a jewel
I keep telling myself, this evening
the weekend
soon, soon, soon

For someone who doesn't drink anymore
I sure do spend a lot of time
looking at the bottle

Ghost

There is a ghost in my house,
and I never see her face, but she
is familiar to me, haunting like a
memory. She hovers as a peripheral
shape, amorphous smoke. Sage
has been smudged, prayers have
been prayed at helplessly desperate
hours, but she remains. I hear her
in the slamming of a door, the
shattering of a glass, an unkindness
whispered against the back of my
neck.

Her ice-pick fingers poke and prod
behind my eyes, dig into the meat
of my shoulders and hold me down,
keep me paralyzed when I wake in the night.
She's been with me all my life,
taking root in so many places I became
a forest floor and now, I don't trust
that I could find the right spot to dig her out.
I can taste her presence like a pill behind
my teeth. I know her name, the warning
of her my racing heart, and I can't seem
to make her leave.

The truth is, I don't know
who I would be without my anger.

Peacekeeper

I've been putting out fires long before
I knew how to make them, long before
I knew they could hurt. I followed the
wake of your inferno, sweeping up
your cinders and making it look like
we had never been there, that you
hadn't just razed an entire coastline.

Now, I'm not perfect. I've destroyed
many a forest thanks to my own
thoughtlessness. I've left candles
burning when I shouldn't, played with
matches and coaxed bonfires to life in
unsafe places, but damn, do I try to fix it
when damage has been done. I've been
blanketing the flames with my own body
for years, and I have the burns to prove it.

Sometimes, I still expect you to realize
what you've done. To turn around, pick
up a broom, administer some burn cream,
plant a fucking tree to replace all those lost
to your anger, but you don't. Maybe that's
my fault. I set the precedent, the expectation
that the mess would be cleaned up one way
or another, so you don't have to look at it.

People always say the definition of insanity

is doing the same thing over and over and
expecting a different result. My therapist
would say "let go or be dragged."
Tell me, is a grip weak or strong for
holding on?

Something About Bravery

There's a girl sitting across from you,
and it's just dinner at a place you've been
a thousand times, but the paint looks different
this evening, and you're so nervous you shake.

You explain it away as a chill in the air, and
she smiles like she doesn't believe you, but
it's a harmless lie so she lets you keep your
secrets, says nothing as you sit on your hands.

She's done this before, and so have you, but
not like this. Not like taking up a table for
three hours, not like discussing your entire
lives, not like wondering about *next times*

before this time is even done. There's a girl
sitting across from you, and it's a secret,
she's a secret, this evening is a whisper of
a thought hidden in your closet, but you're

here, and maybe that says something about
bravery. Maybe this secret tells you more
about yourself than you thought. At this point,
you've always been calculating the fastest

way back to your car, smile tight and say
goodnight before they get any bright ideas.
But her eyes are bright and knowing as you

try to fit one more topic into your goodbye.

She brushes your hair behind your ear, *classic*,
and *this* you've done before, but not like this.
It should be simple, but you're just a girl with
a closet of secrets, and you're not actually brave.

Deprivation

Movements are slow and hazy,
careful as I gauge my steadiness.
I feel drunk, conscious of my sway
but unable to right myself. The mental
orders I give of "stand up straight,
walk normal" don't seem to reach
my limbs. Behind my glasses, I'm
blinking away the blurriness. The
world is viewed through a pinhole,
black crowding the edges of my vision.
My body doesn't know how to be alert
anymore.

My mind has been a prized thing,
celebrated for its stretch and reach,
the ease at which it grasps something,
but its fingers are no longer dextrous.
I've adjusted well to the chore of thought,
the effort it takes to string sentences
together, reconnect tongue to brain and
provide the illusion that I am any sort of
alive. I count days on one hand and
hours of sleep on the other, and
neither number gets high.

I stare at my tired reflection and wonder
if I've ever had any other kind of eyes.

Shed

You know,
I can no longer pinpoint the moment
I stopped being afraid. It feels like I've
always lived with this suffocating fear,
like a pillow over my face, and I grew
so used to the strain of breathing. I'd
spent so long twisting myself into a more
desirable shape, drowning in fabric, in
smiles, in opinions and kindness that
crippled me more than anything else.
I wondered when I could relax into my own
skin, but even that didn't feel like mine
anymore.

I know that hurt precedes the healing.
I remember the growing pains, a body
on fire, curling towards change
everyone promised would be worth it
one day. I understand that I've been
misshapen so long that untwisting
will feel like a bone rebroken to set
properly, but I've always had a handle
on my pain.

Letting someone love me was like
peeling an orange apart to scrape away
all my bitterness. Loving myself bade me
take stock of my wooden form, and carve

myself beautiful, whittling away lies and
worthlessness. I ripped myself free from
the chrysalis. I forgave the mess I was.

I am sloughing off layers of guilt and doubt
and skin, the hanging viscera of my antlers
as I shed my velvet, until I am pink
and glistening as a newborn. This fresh
creation of myself is tender, but *oh,*
I will be so bright, after.

I will be so strong.

The Gardener

I've tried for years, but I can only
sporadically keep plants alive. They
thrive for a few weeks without change in
routine, and suddenly the leaves yellow.
The blooms shrivel and die.
I replace them when I can, but I know
their lives will be short-lived. However,
there is a garden I tend to with such care
that I keep it secret from prying eyes,
each vibrant flower a petal-perfect memory.

When your own garden was plagued
with sickness, I watched you dig through
the rotted remains looking for any sign
of life. Elbow deep in the muck and
nothing to show for it. For months,
you wouldn't leave your garden, sitting
amongst the filth, breathing in decay
like everything would sprout again
if you believed long and hard enough.
I gave you flowers from my secret
garden, couldn't bear to see you like
that. I would select a bloom with care
and offer it to you, just to watch you
toss it onto the diseased pile, like you
thought it would take root all on its own,
no nurturing needed.

My flowers didn't grow easily; they were
a product of hard work and hard love, but
I kept giving them to you, and you kept tossing
them onto the pile of slowly corroding stems,
and I'm sorry, but I realized one day, I had
nothing left to give. I needed time to regrow,
to coax my garden into bloom once more.
Today, I showed up on your doorstep with a small
bud in hand. It's been a while, and I still can't seem
to help it—the act of giving myself away is second
nature—but I knew things would be different this
time. There was potting soil on your back porch.

Resonance

I remember the first time I ever went to Pride
in my town. I'd never seen a gathering like it
with so many avenues of self-expression,
so many colors. I wore mine, hidden under my
flannel shirt, like that wasn't already a dead
give away. I was a private person by choice
and by self-preservation, but as the sun sank,
I grew bold. I unbuttoned my shirt.

I don't remember what it was that drew me to her.
Maybe she walked with a confidence I didn't yet
know. Maybe it was the group she walked with in
the parade, specifics long since forgotten. But
I remember her hair, dark and wavy with June heat.
Her smile, infectious. Her energy had snagged me,
pulled me to the barricade. By some intimate design,
she walked over, put her hand on my cheek and
her lips on the other, and then she was gone.

A thirty second encounter burrowed under my
skin. She probably doesn't remember the girl
in purple and pink and blue, combat boots,
braided hair under a ballcap, glitter on her eyes,
and full of nerves. Maybe I was one of many kisses.
I'll never know exactly what it was that compelled
her away from the march to brand me, but
something in our blood was singing the same
song that night. A chorus of souls ringing out
in the dark of Houston. *You are not alone.*

A Language Which Needs No Words

I think about the redwoods in California,
the sheer breadth and height of them
farfetched even with picture proof, and
you have to be there to really believe it.

I think of how fungi can communicate with
itself from opposite sides of a forest, giving warnings
of disease or directions of growth for the best
nutrients, but it's all the same mycelium.

I think about the arts and how they speak a
language which needs no words. How we
send music into space on the off-chance
something else is out there listening.

I think about movement on a canvas, the
chalk depiction of a ballerina, the secretive
smile of a woman, how Aivazovsky paints
the sea. Michaelangelo sees bodies in marble

before he ever takes a chisel to it. Truth climbs
from her well, naked and outraged; Liberty leads
the people; the Wanderer faces the sublime.
I think of how people pause in a museum

and how it's the same as someone stopping

to hold a blooming moonflower, how we love to
soak in the rain, or watch the sunset; how we find
little ways to echo art and majesty in our own lives.

I see the visible veins in my skin like a lightning
bolt, the bruise of a constellation under my eyes,
Aphrodite folds of my skin. I equate myself to what
astounds me, because if I find it all so beautiful

then surely, I must be too.

Second Shadow

There is a frailty that precedes death;
the skeleton is never so observable in its
casing as it is in the days before you die.
Then, there's the speed at which one
deteriorates, a boulder picking up pace
as it hurtles down the mountain. One day,
you might be talking, eating, drinking.
The next, your awareness is nothing but
pain, and breathing is a fight you don't
have strength for.

I do not know what it is to live to old age,
to house sickness in your own body.
I have not mourned my independence,
become reliant on others to speak for me.
To pronounce me *too tired*, to be the reason
the gathering ends. My skin has not
gone papery-thin, blue veins pulsing like
a beacon for nurses. Endless nurses. I
have never clung to my faith, desperately
trying to trust when I am at my lowest
point, and I have never had to grapple with
the question, "is it worth it to keep me alive?"

I may understand pain, but mine is not
a pain that will kill me. My aches are
not a side-effect of the end; I don't have
to question the symptoms of my discomfort.

But this also means that I forget to be
grateful that I am alive. There have been
times where Death was not a passive
character in my life. He sat beside me
in the car, patient and wondering if
I would make that choice. If I would
jerk the wheel. He does not encourage
or frighten me into action. He does not
loom over me with his scythe held aloft,
but I have seen his presence like a second
shadow. He has sat in the corner of my room,
waiting for me to turn out the light.

It's been a while since I've seen him.
He has been banished to the back seat,
to the back of the room, so far removed
from me that I forget he is there. He has
heard my laughter and my joy, and he
follows, always follows, because he is
inevitable. But the sun does not shine on
him, does not make him stretch into twilight,
does not make him blanket my world. Even
in the glow of a candle where shadows are
strongest, he cannot yet reach out to snuff
the flame.

Your Hands on the Dial

We're always sharing music.
I play mine low in case you're
not feeling the genre, but you
ask me to turn it up. You tell me I
have good taste. You walk in the
door from work, sans greeting,
and request a song. Your newest
hyperfocus, the track that got you
through a hard shift, just something
you think I'll enjoy. I love the way
you invite me into your mind.
This is what I'm liking right now.
Share this with me.
Are you feeling it?
Yeah, me too.

I keep thinking of that song;
you know the one. It's not
constant, not playing in a feedback
loop in my head, lyrics repeating
endlessly, even though we asked
Alexa to repeat it. Several times.
That's not how I think of it anymore.
I think of it as a setting: The couch,
exposed but private. I think of it as
a time: Evening, dark and damp with
rain. A tempo: Polyrhythmic, keeping
us on the edge. That song is gooseflesh,

it's a deep breath and deeper exhale
at the summoning of a memory. It's a fist
around my spine and brandishing
me like a sword, gorgeous and Named
and powerful. That song is a touch:
My thumb on your lip, holding your
gaze with more than my eyes, and
your hands pressing bone-white
into my hips, your hands on the dial,
turning it up. I can't listen to that
song anymore without hearing
you over the music. Without
feeling your fingertip shiver
at the crease of my knees.

Legacy

I still remember the heavy feeling of
coins tumbling into the cup of my palm.
Once my father's, they now belong to me.
Seven drachmas that I keep squirreled away
in an old jewelry box, like a woman guarding
her sacred pearls. I ran my fingers over them,
tracing Greek letters around their beveled edge,
shapes and words foreign to me. But I've always
been hungry for understanding.

When my father was a young man, he went
to Greece with his church. It baffles me
that he does not look fondly on that trip,
but his heart is landlocked and mine is a bird
poised for freefall and flight. He returned with
the coins, with a photo album rarely thumbed
through, both crumbs of experience that I
gorged myself on like a starving, stray dog.
I ran my thumb around the edge of those
coins so many times I can still feel the embossed
letters against my skin.

I spent hours the night they were given to me
decoding the characters as if they would reveal
some great secret of the universe, not just a name.
But I researched the name, the city, the country,
until the sun had risen and I'd eaten my fill
of newness. Sometimes, I admit that hunger

is a misnomer. I am not so willing to lay
myself bare, the red cavern of my chest
pulsing and empty, begging to be filled.
It seems I have always been looking for
some part of him in myself. His humor,
his kindness, his heart. The history of
where he has been and what he has done–
what he can do—so that, one day, I might hear
you are so like him.

I suppose it's why I reach for his guitar today,
strings leaving tenderness like golden coins.

Roman Empire

Sometimes, it's barely anything at all.
Just a shifting of the fingers that
reveals a book's dedication. It's a
private war publicly fought because
something was taken from you, and
it left you with such a hole that nothing
remains but a rage and righteousness
so feral they put the black storms at sea
to shame.

Other times it is "Just hold me,"
and "I don't want you to change."
Maybe it is the flexing of a hand
after you touch her skin for the
first time. Maybe it's a claim so biblical
it scars, Song of Solomon 8:6 brought
to life. It is "Oh Captain, my Captain,"
and boys standing on tables in salute.
It is the sweeping crescendo of strings
and keys, and air into a pipe,
Flying and lullabies from fauns
and *Test Drive*, and *Enterprising
Young Men.*

It's a kiss held apart by glass.
It is άριστος Αχαιωύ, best of the Greeks,
and "what has Hector ever done to me?"
It is vengeance built on kings and patience,

prison stones counted but never named.
It is returning to Dust and returning to
each other. "No harm ever came from
reading a book," or reading a book to Life.
It's dancing with the devil so skillfully
you and he begin to blur, and you were
helpless to it—you should hate it but you don't,
so over the cliff's edge you go, together.

I wrap leather around my wrist, imitating
the bracelet of a boy who can pluck things
from his dreams, when I need his bravery.
I put braids in my hair like a Shieldmaiden's,
clothe myself in shoes and jackets and rings
of those I need to borrow something from.
A little fire in my blood, a little strength. The
courage not to run away. I indulge in good food
because I am worthy of more than survival.
I am an amalgamation of every character
that has felt the smallest bit like looking in a mirror.
My skin is decorated with the constant reminder
that I contain multitudes. Have I ever consumed
something that did not, in turn, consume me?

There are a thousand tiny ways
I am loved

In the way he kisses me before he eats mushrooms
In the way my dog puts her leg over my lap
In the way my presence is wanted
She would love this, she should be here,
Let's take her with us
My friend calls me the coolest person she knows
My friend calls me brave
My friend holds my hand and grieves with me
We screech and wheeze with laughter over sushi
And yes
I have my mother's cackle
But I'm not ashamed of it anymore
Her laughter is pure and loud and alive
She tells me I'm funny
My father calls me a good daughter
A good person
He's proud of me
My brother is generous, a heart of giving that bleeds
And is fiercely protected
But he lets me see past the armor
He lets me See him

There are a thousand tiny ways I am loved

Dear Younger Me

Dear younger me,
At fourteen, your innocent heart will have
innocent problems. Hold onto the moments
where your biggest concern is not knowing
the right words. One day, they will come as
easy as breathing.

Dear younger me,
I know you are wounded, but you don't
have to lie. You're seventeen. You're not
old enough to be so burdened, to be this tired.
The truth is not your enemy, but it's so much easier
to leave her out. No one is listening anyway,
what's the harm in another lie? Yes, I'm getting
enough sleep, yes, I've had enough to eat.
I'm so full, really.

Dear younger me,
Do you ever get tired of crying? Twenty-one
and constantly on the edge—no one has talked
you down in months. Your chest is a collapsing
star, and you've gotten really good at hiding the
damage, even better at seeing the lack of it in
others. Remember that time you witnessed
two people in the throes of shrieking laughter,
that kind of joy unbridled and wild and a
stranger to you? You don't even pray anymore,
but do you remember how you called to God?

Please, one day let it be me.

Dear younger me,
She's intimidating, I know. This mountain,
the Stone Lady before you, a rock of judgment and
condemnation. You're twenty-three—never done
anything like this before—and the size of her says
not today. You can't do it.
But your stubbornness is working in your favor,
And that climb aches like nothing you've ever
known. It's worth it, to be cleaved apart
like that, to discard those words and those fears
long-nurtured as they were and heavy with
protection. You may be weeping in the shadow
of her staircase, but the midday sun awaits you,
and he will dry your tears.

Dear younger me,
You won't have much money,
or any furniture, really, but you'll
have him. You'll be twenty-five,
you'll have your own place,
and before anything else,
you'll have laughter to fill the
rooms so it already feels like home.

Dear younger me,
I told you the words would come
easier. I told you it would be like
breathing, like an exhale that slots
the words into place, a story finished
at twenty-nine that took you the entire year to

write. Tell me it doesn't feel like purpose
realized, this weight of your own creation.
Tell me there isn't magic in you.